ARTIST TRANSCRIPTIONS PIANO

CHARLIE PARKER FOR PIANO
featuring
The Paul Smith Trio

T0081498

Transcribed by Forrest "Woody" Mankowski

ISBN-13: 978-1-4234-1923-5
ISBN-10: 1-4234-1923-5

HAL•LEONARD®
CORPORATION

7777 W. BLUEMOUND RD. P.O. BOX 13819 MILWAUKEE, WI 53213

In Australia contact:
Hal Leonard Australia Pty. Ltd.
4 Lentara Court
Cheltenham, Victoria, 3192 Australia
Email: ausadmin@halleonard.com.au

Visit Hal Leonard Online at
www.halleonard.com

Moose the Mooche

By Charlie Parker

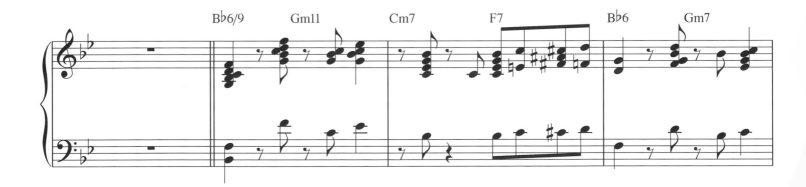

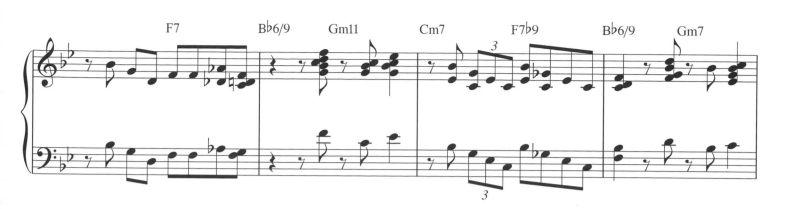

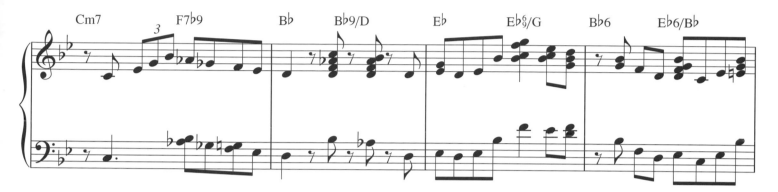

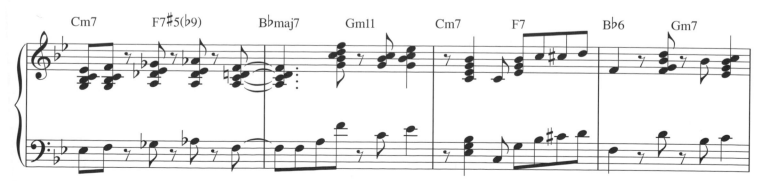

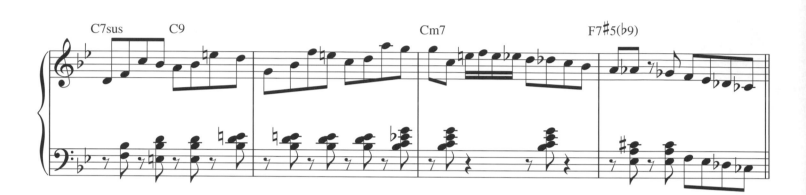

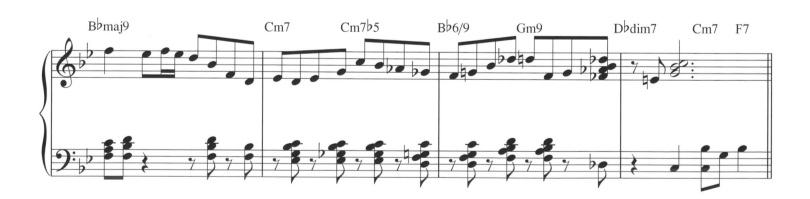

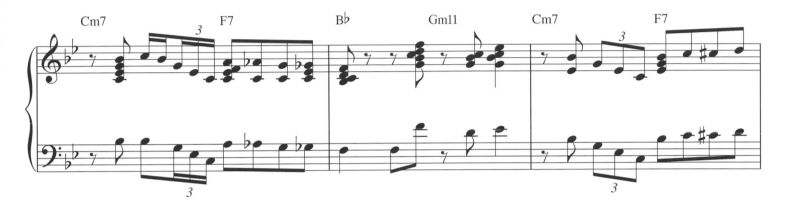

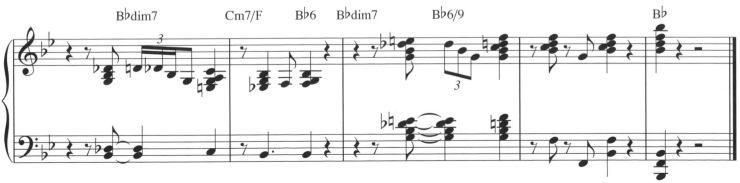

My Little Suede Shoes

By Charlie Parker

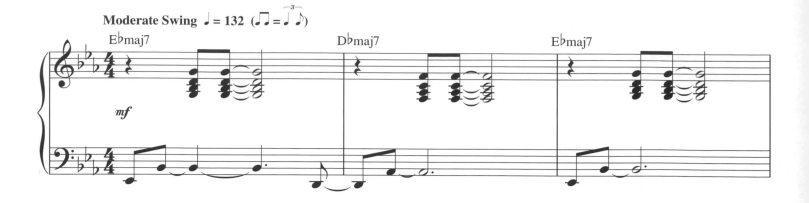

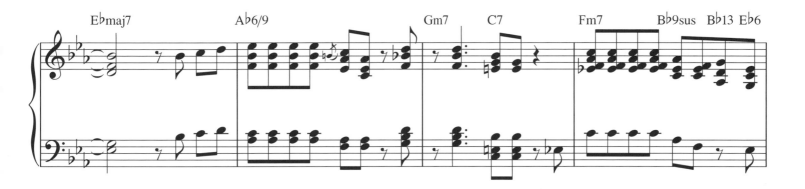

To Coda ⊕

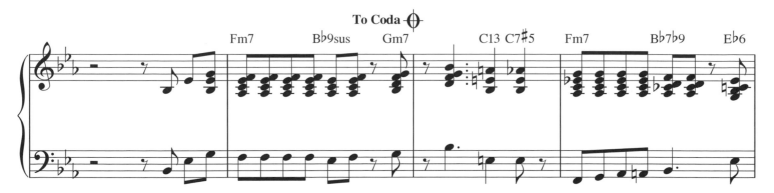

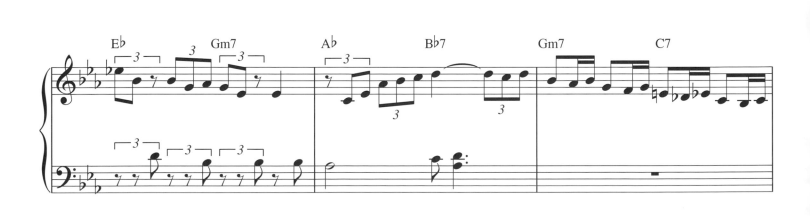

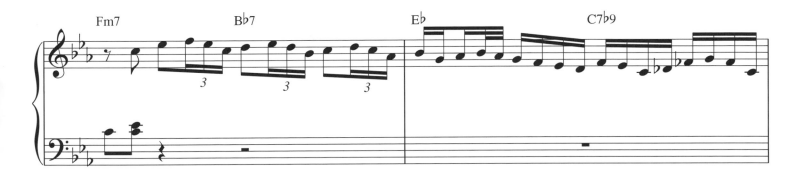

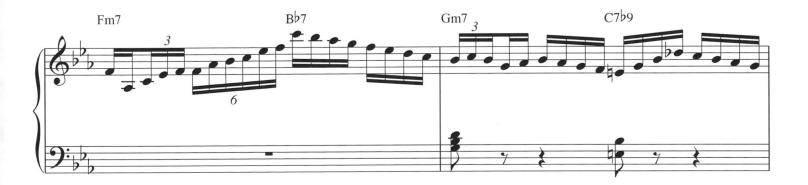

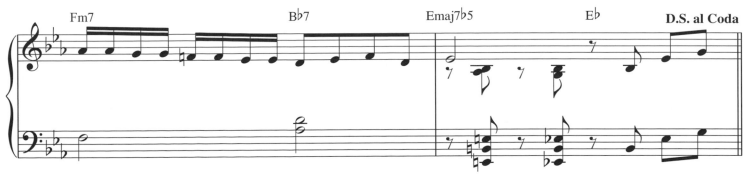

D.S. al Coda

CODA

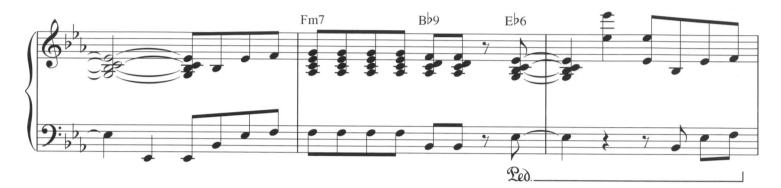

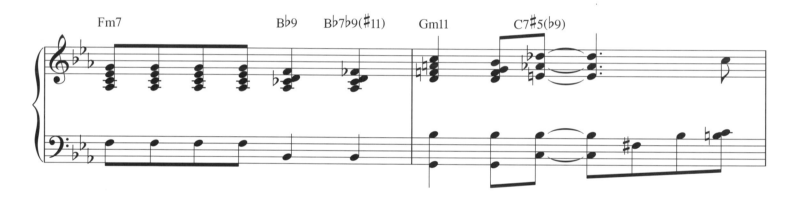

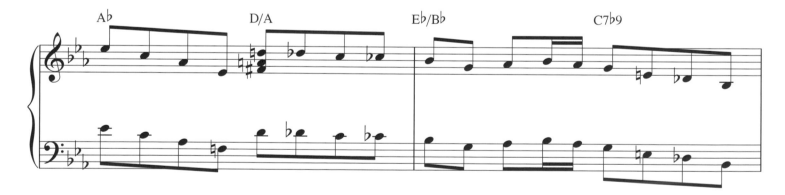

Visa

By Charlie Parker

To Coda ⊕

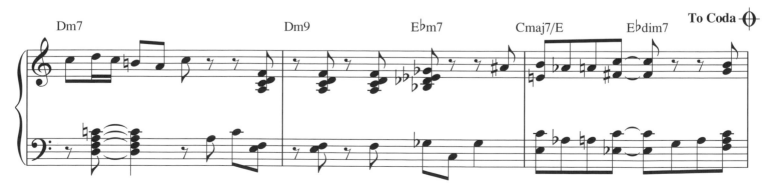

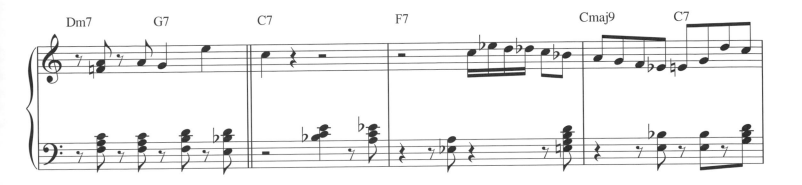

(Begin trading 4's with bass)

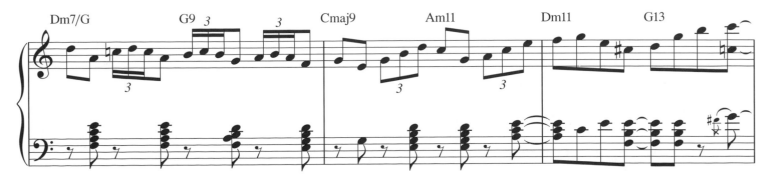

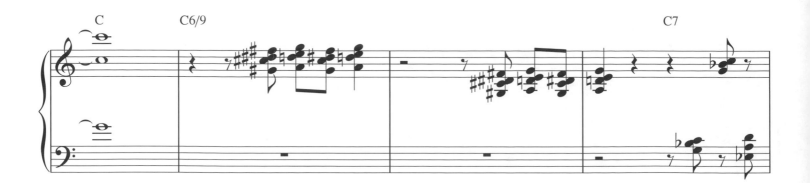

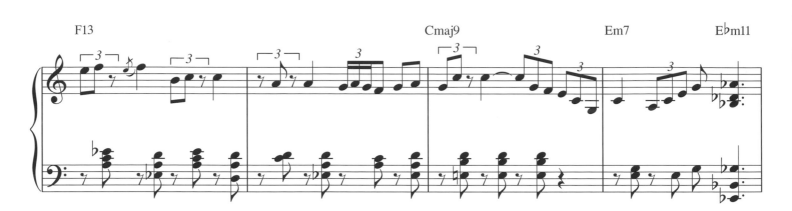

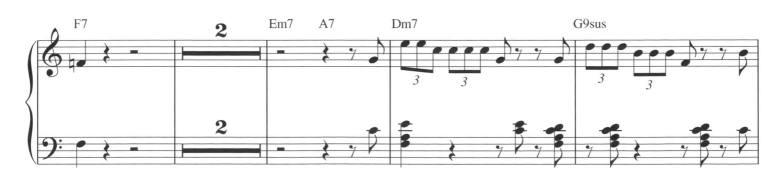

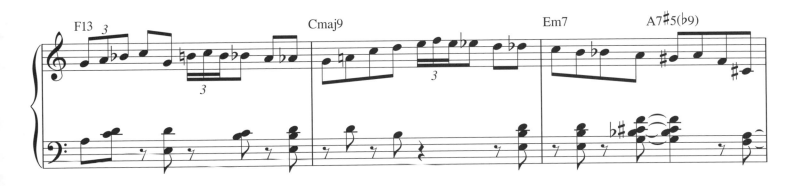

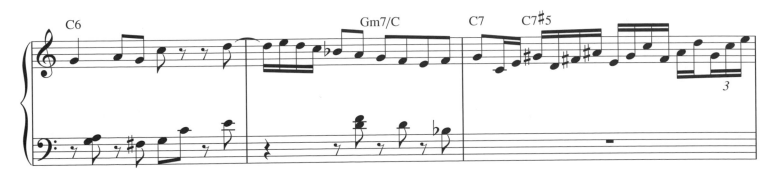

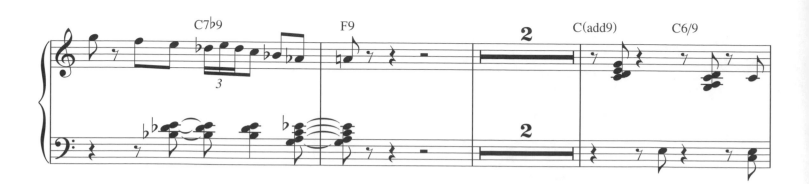

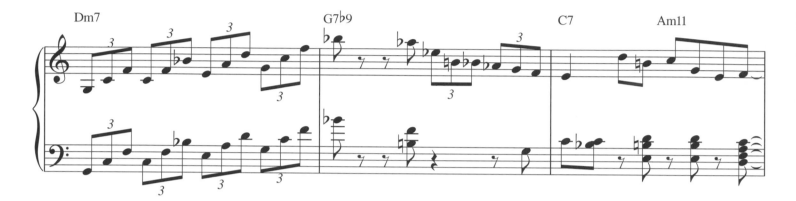

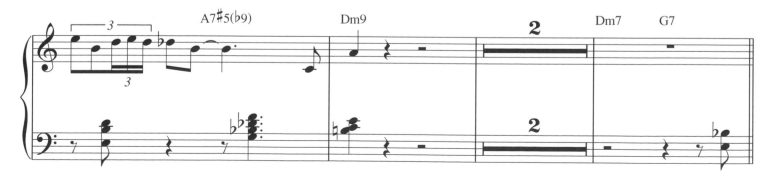

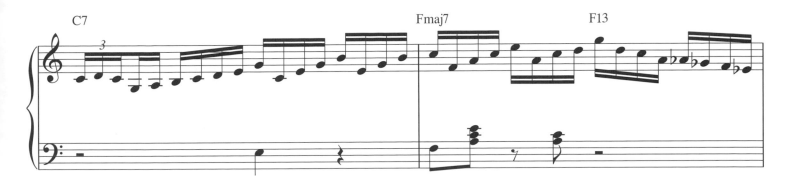

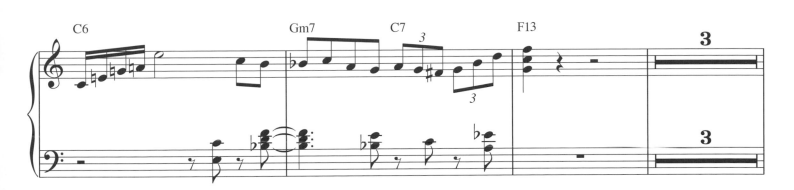

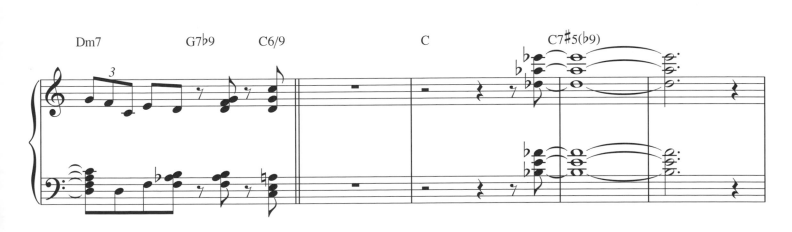

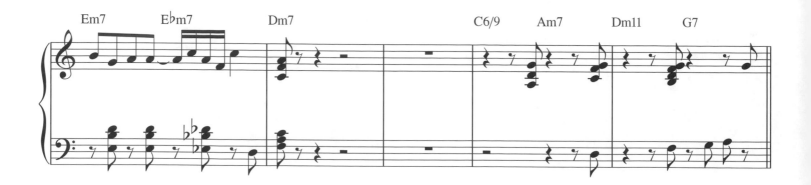

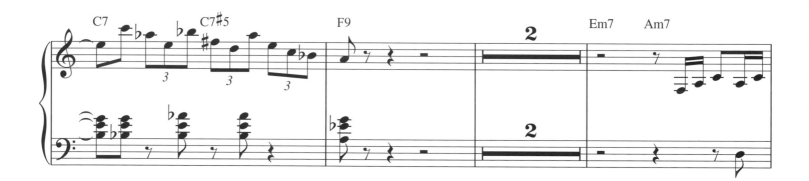

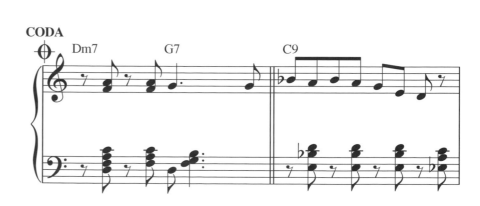

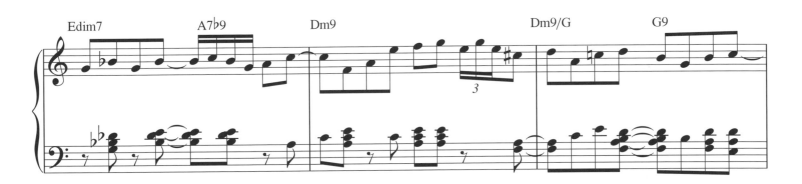

Chi Chi

By Charlie Parker

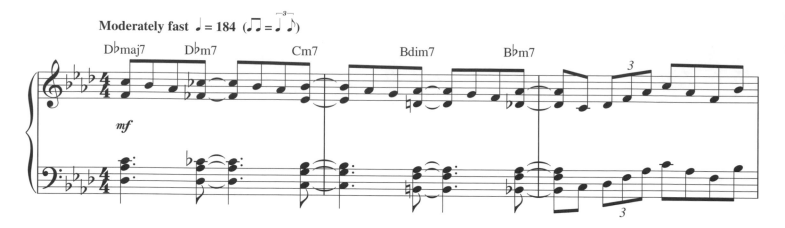

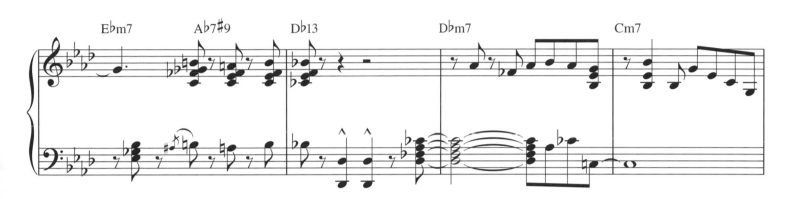

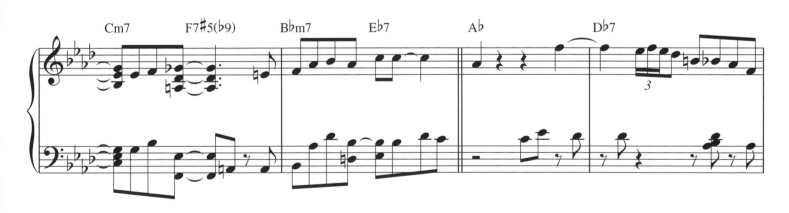

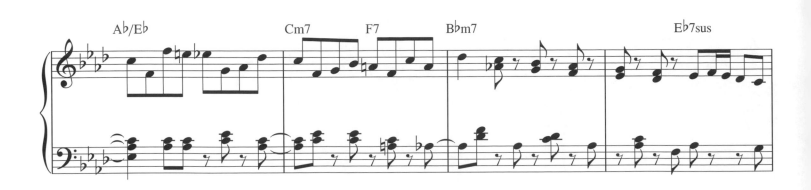

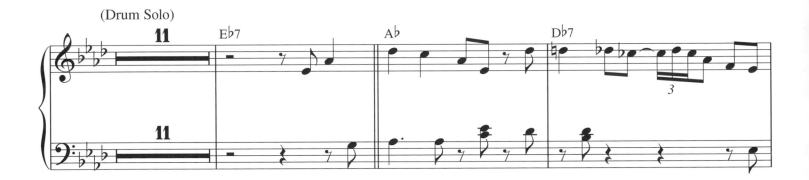

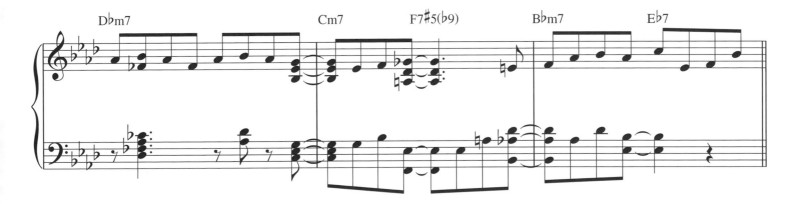

Confirmation

By Charlie Parker

Bright Swing ♩ = 202

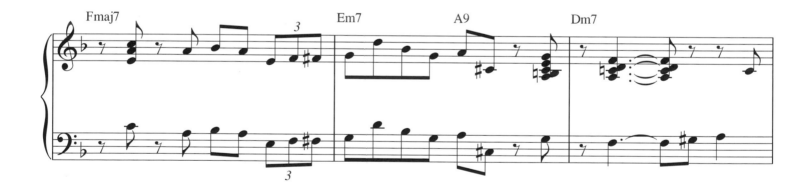

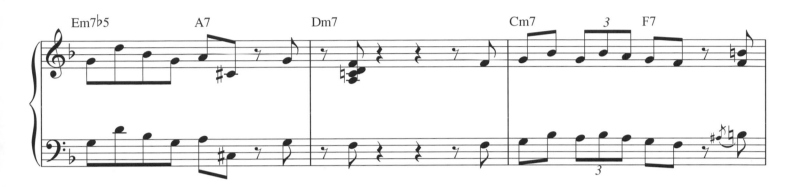

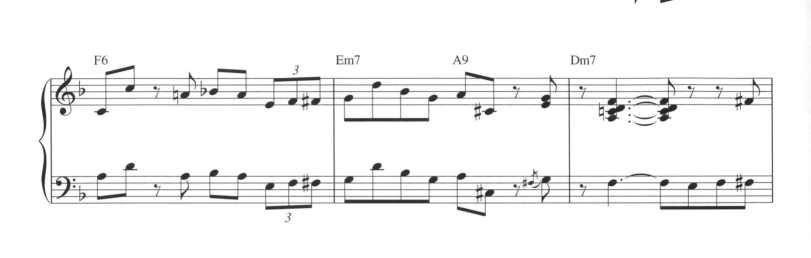

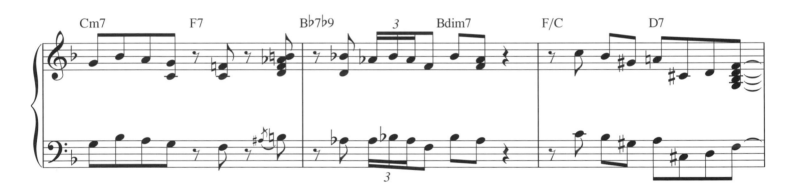

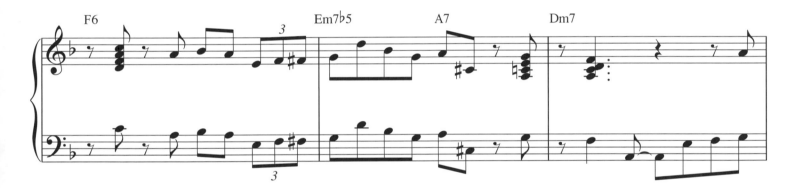

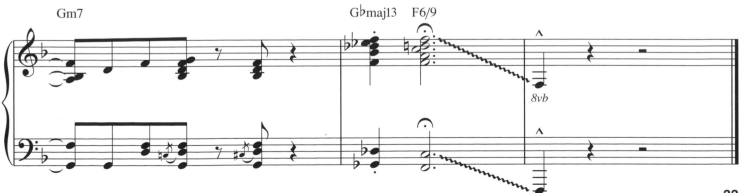

Yardbird Suite

By Charlie Parker

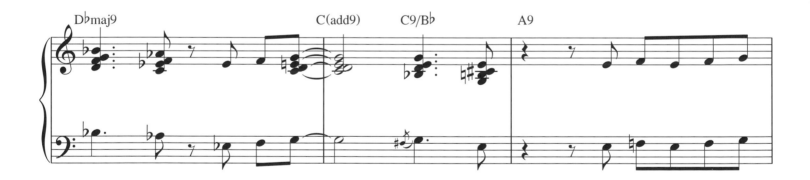

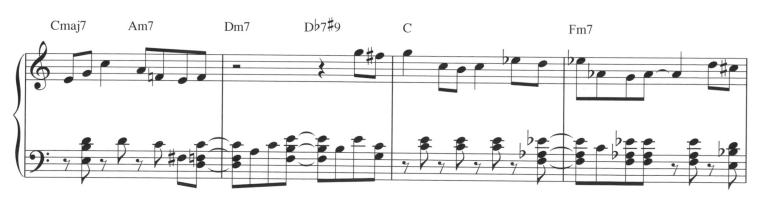

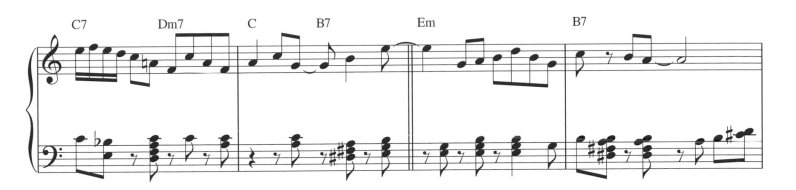

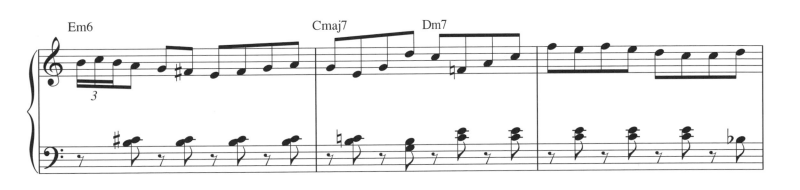

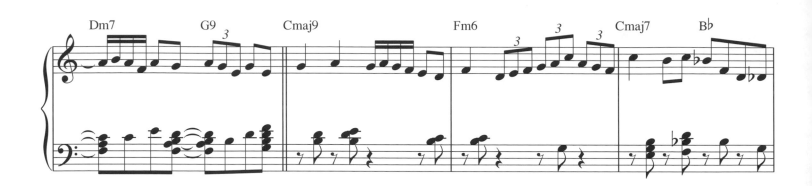

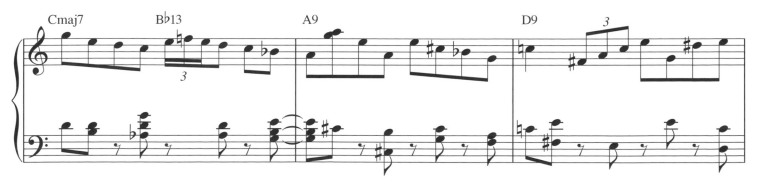

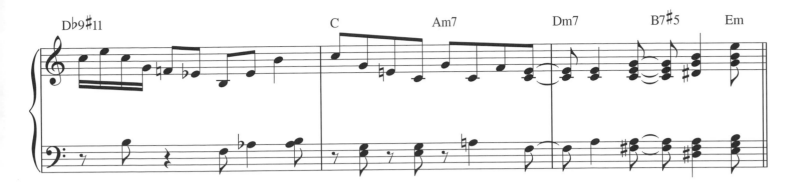

Back Home Blues

By Charlie Parker

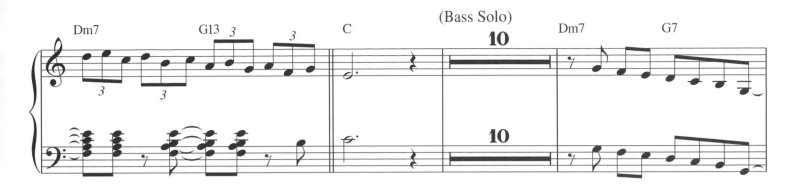

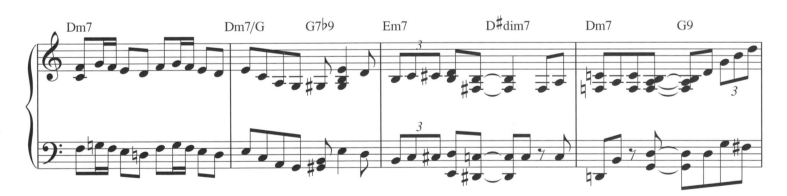

Ornithology

By Charlie Parker and Bennie Harris

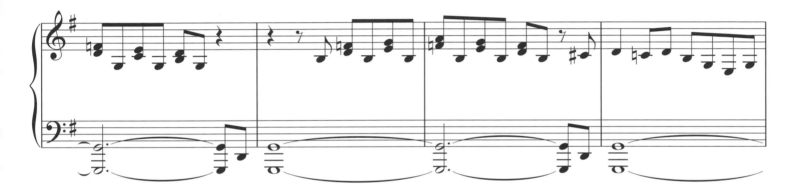

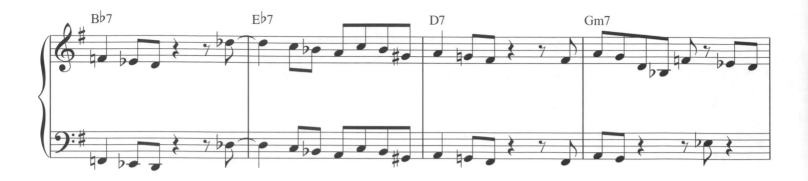

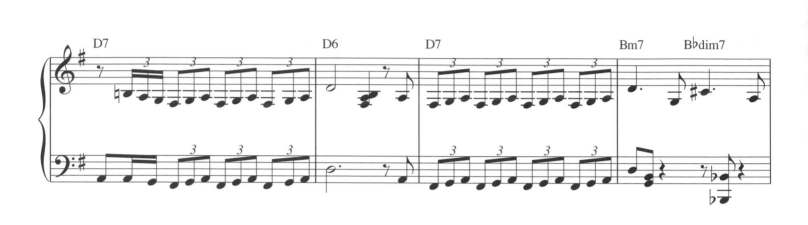

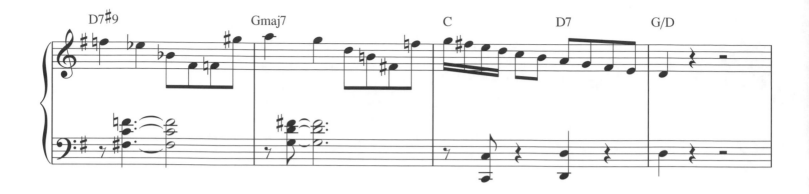

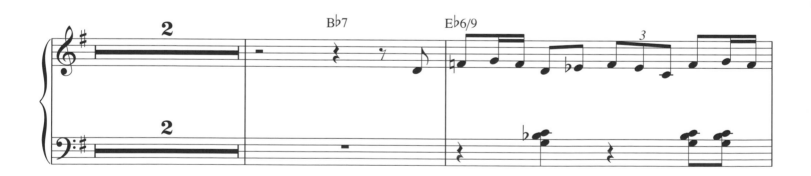

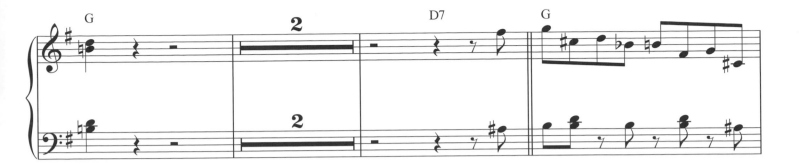

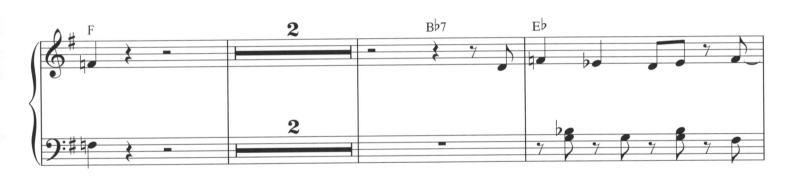

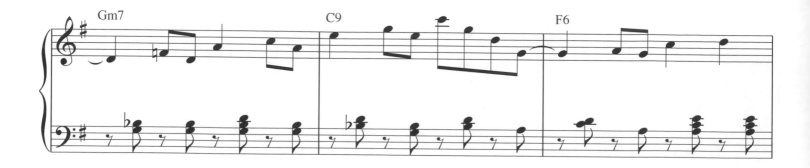

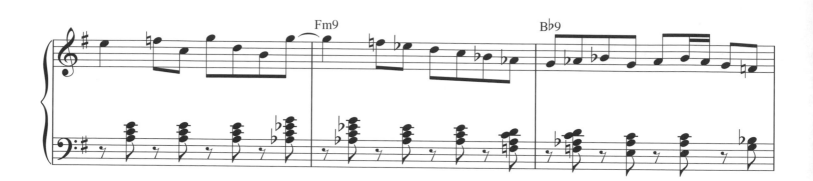

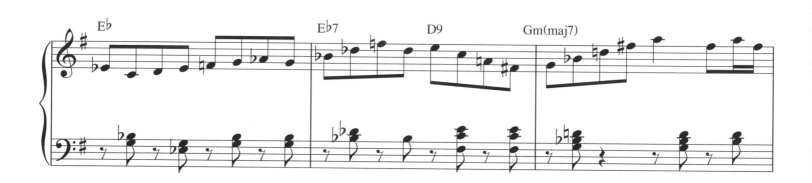

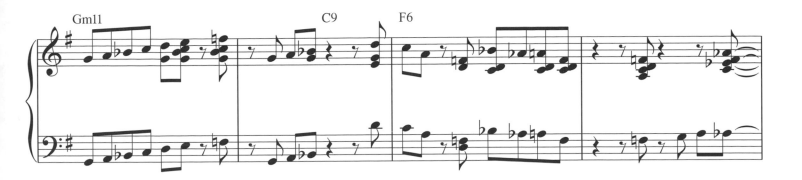

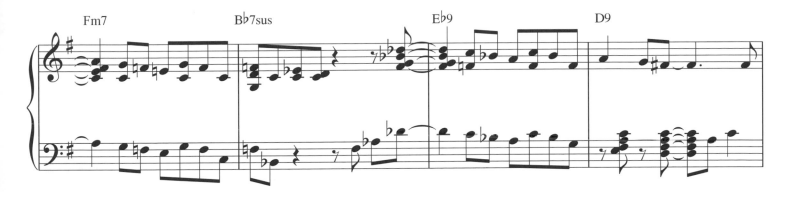

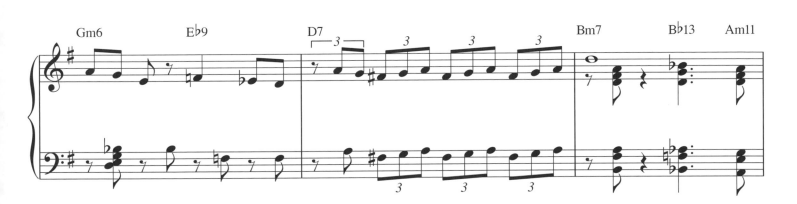

Segment

By Charlie Parker

Moderately fast ♩ = 216

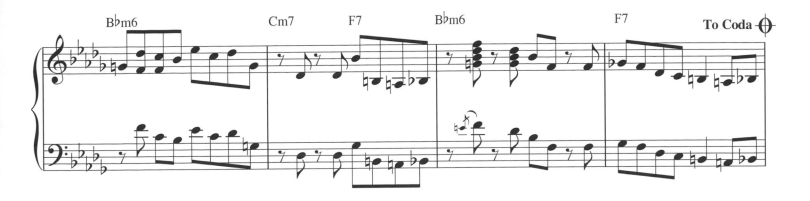

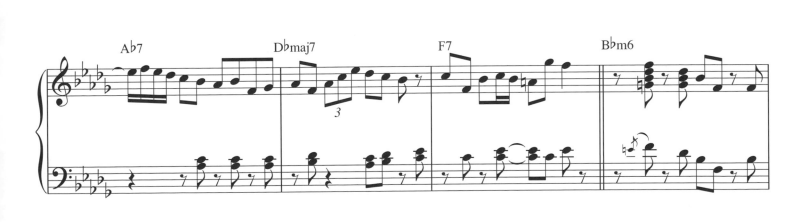

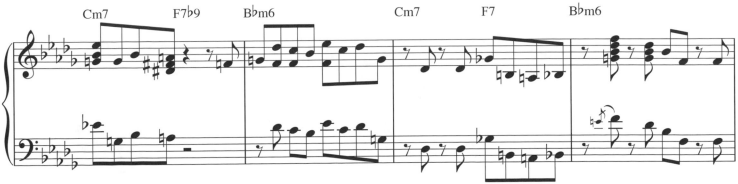

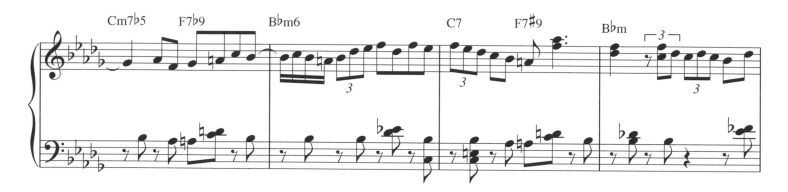

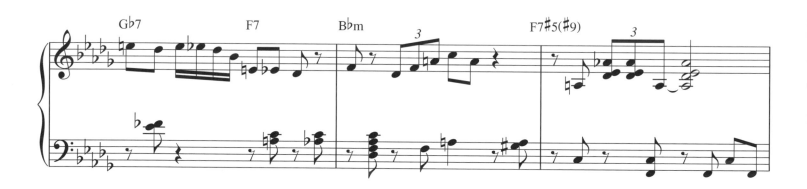

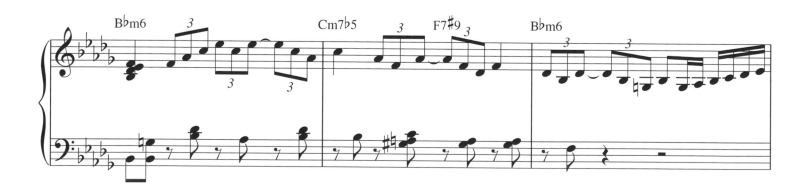

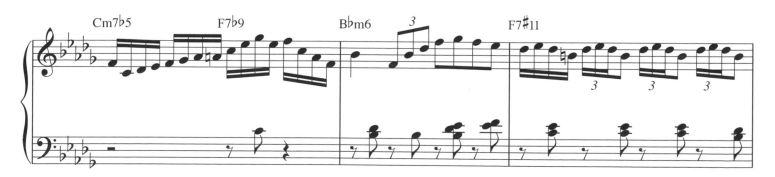

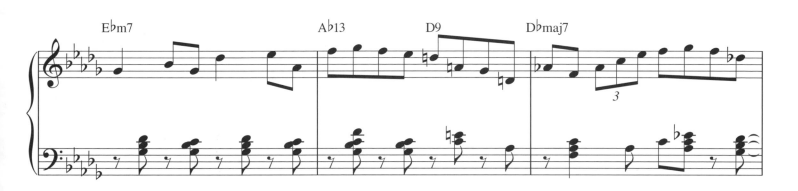

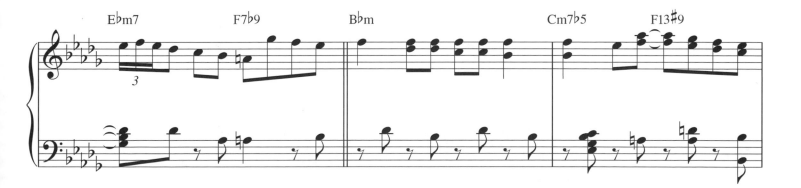

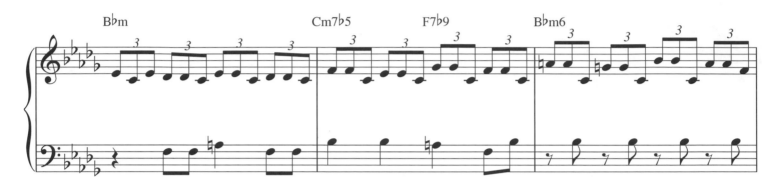

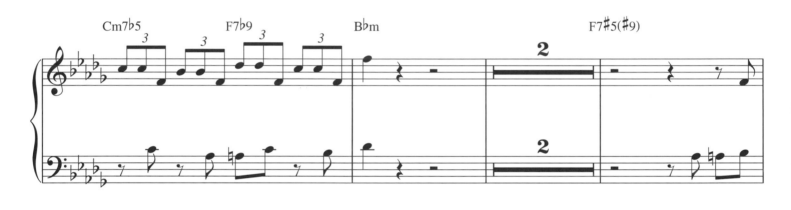

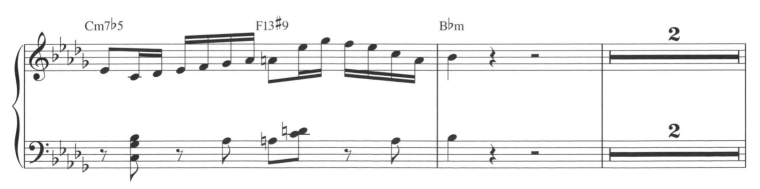

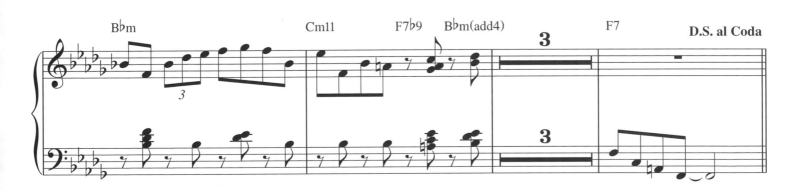

Blues for Alice

By Charlie Parker

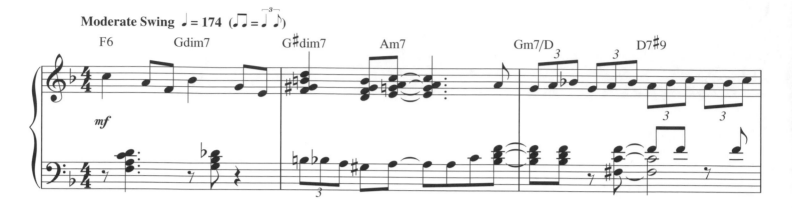

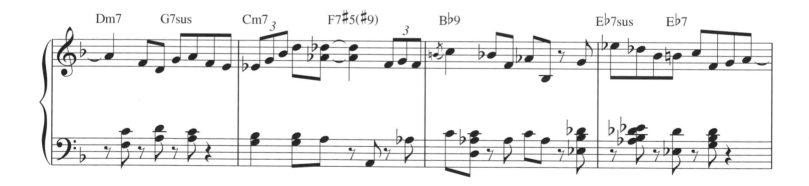

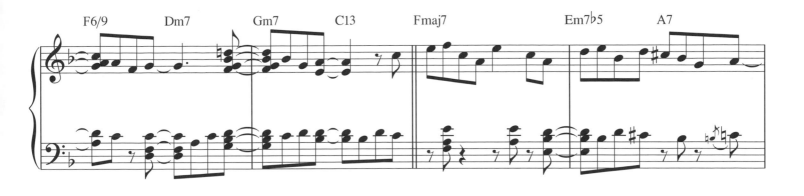

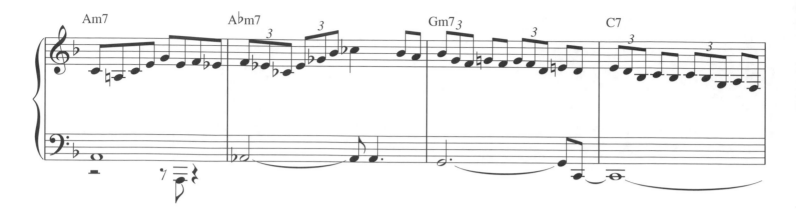

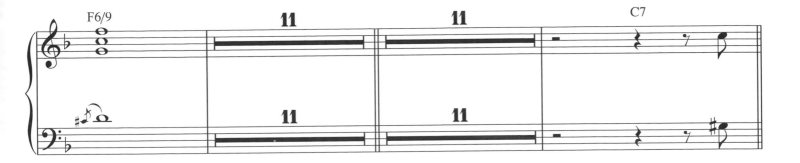

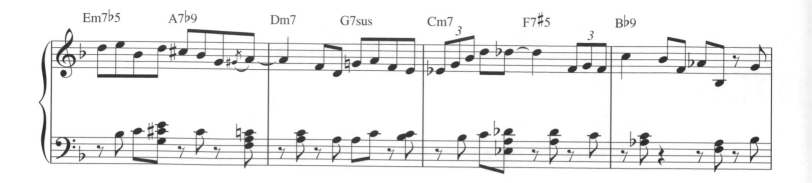

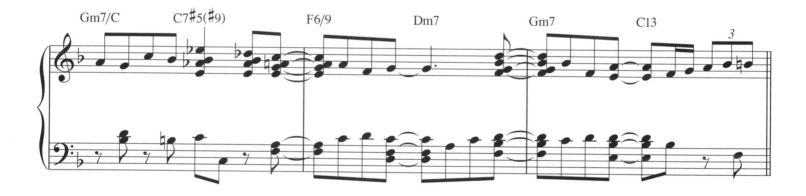

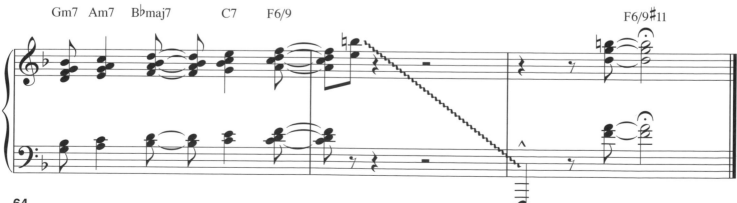

Au Privave

By Charlie Parker

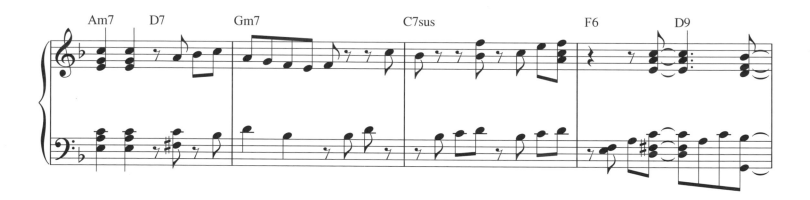

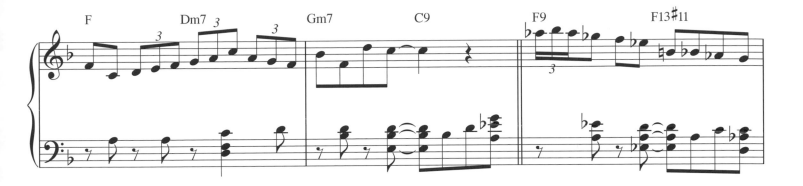

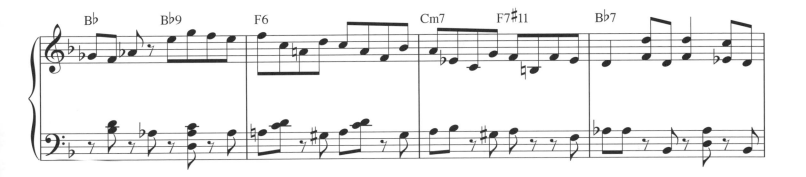

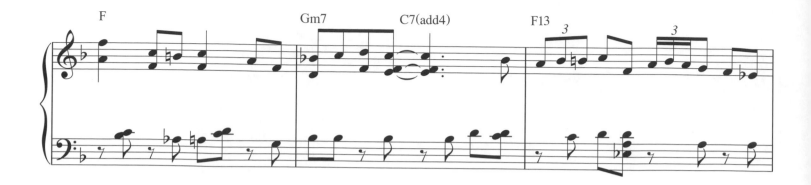

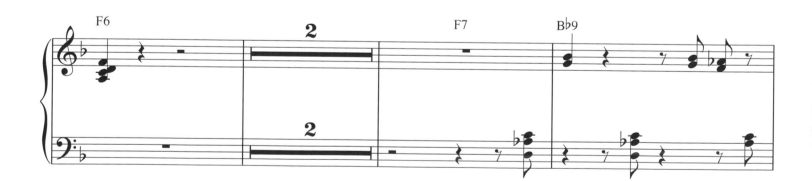

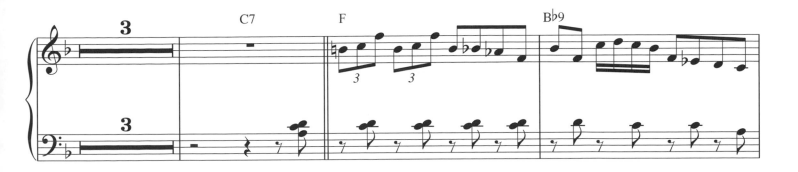

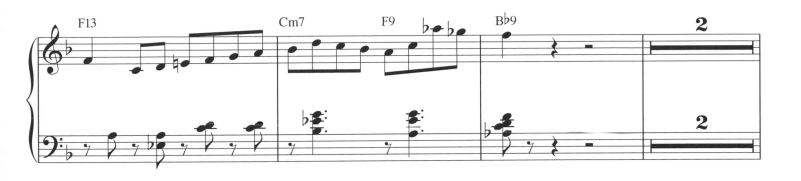

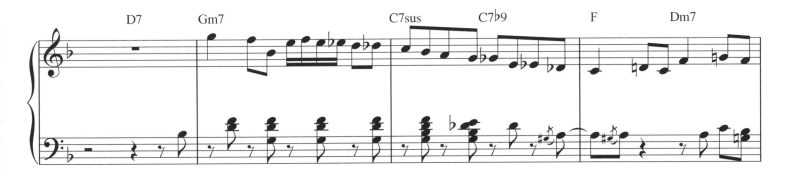

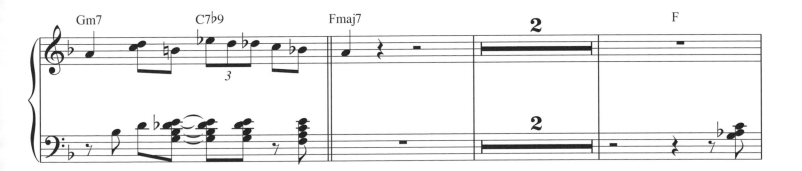

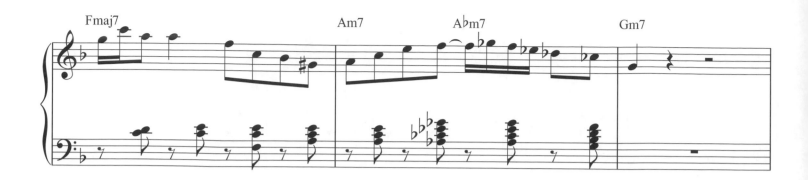

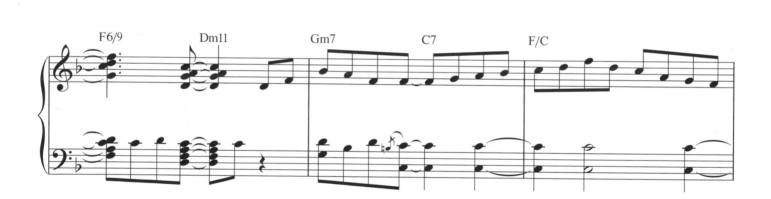